GIGGLES and GROANS

BEANO books
geddes & grosset

HOW MANY
PSYCHIATRISTS
DOES IT TAKE TO
CHANGE
A LIGHTBULB?
JUST ONE,
BUT THE LIGHTBULB
HAS TO REALLY
WANT TO
CHANGE!

CHUCKLE
CHUCKLE!

HA-HA-HA!

WHY SHOULD YOU TAKE A PENCIL TO BED?
TO DRAW THE CURTAINS!

HA-HA-HA!

WHY DID THE MAN RUN AROUND HIS BED?
TO CATCH UP ON HIS SLEEP!

HA-HA-HA!

WHAT DID ONE VOLCANO SAY TO THE OTHER?
DO YOU LAVA ME LIKE I LAVA YOU?

TEE-HEE!

WHAT GOES UP AND DOES NOT COME DOWN?
YOUR AGE.

HA-HA-HA!

WHY DID THE BOY TIPTOE PAST THE MEDICINE CABINET?
HE DIDN'T WANT TO WAKE THE SLEEPING PILLS!

TEE-HEE!

WHAT STARTS WITH A P, ENDS WITH AN E, AND HAS A MILLION LETTERS IN IT?
POST OFFICE!

HEE-HEE!

WHAT IS THE DIFFERENCE BETWEEN A JEWELLER AND A JAILER?
A JEWELLER SELLS WATCHES AND A JAILER WATCHES CELLS!

HEE-HEE!

HA-HA-HA!

WHO STOLE THE SOAP?
THE ROBBER DUCK!
TEE-HEE!
WHAT IS BIG, RED AND EATS ROCKS?
A BIG RED ROCK EATER!
TEE-HEE!
WHAT HAS FOUR LEGS BUT DOESN'T MOVE?
A TABLE!
HEE-HEE!
WHO WAS BIGGER, MR. BIGGER OR HIS SON?
HIS SON . . . HE WAS A LITTLE BIGGER!
WHAT IS H2O4?
DRINKING!

WHAT DID ONE TONSIL SAY TO THE OTHER
TONSIL?
GET DRESSED UP, THE DOCTOR IS TAKING US OUT!

HEE-HEE!

WHAT DO ALEXANDER THE GREAT AND KERMIT
THE FROG HAVE IN COMMON?
THE SAME MIDDLE NAME!

TEE-HEE!

SNIGGER!

15

CHORTLE! CHORTLE!

WHAT BOW CAN'T BE TIED?
A RAINBOW!

TEE-HEE!

WHAT IS GREEN AND HAS YELLOW WHEELS?
GRASS . . . I LIED ABOUT THE WHEELS!

**WHAT DO YOU CALL A MAN WHO CROSSES A
RIVER TWICE AND DOESN'T TAKE A BATH?**
A DIRTY DOUBLE CROSSER!

HOW DO YOU MAKE ANTIFREEZE?
HIDE HER NIGHTGOWN!

CHUCKLE CHUCKLE CHUCKLE!
TEE-HEE!
WHAT DO YOU GET WHEN YOU CROSS FROSTY THE SNOWMAN WITH A VAMPIRE?
FROSTBITE!

WHAT HAPPENED TO THE ANGRY RABBIT?
IT WAS HOPPING MAD.

WHICH MONKEY WAS DEFEATED AT WATERLOO?

NAPOLEON BABOONAPARTE.

SNIGGER-SNIGGER!

WHY CAN'T YOUR NOSE BE 12 INCHES LONG?
BECAUSE THEN IT WOULD BE A FOOT!

DOES YOUR SHIRT
HAVE HOLES IN IT?
NO,
THEN HOW DID
YOU PUT IT ON?

CHORTLE!

WHAT HAPPENS IF YOU EAT YEAST AND SHOE POLISH?
EVERY MORNING YOU'LL RISE AND SHINE!

SNIGGER-SNIGGER!

HOW MANY BOOKS CAN YOU PUT IN AN EMPTY SCHOOL BAG?
ONE! AFTER THAT IT'S NOT EMPTY!

HA-HA-HA!

HEE-HEE!

WHAT WASHES UP ON VERY SMALL BEACHES?
MICROWAVES!

WHICH WEIGHS MORE, A TON OF FEATHERS
OR A TON OF BRICKS?
NEITHER, THEY BOTH WEIGH A TON!

BASH STREET KIDS JOKES

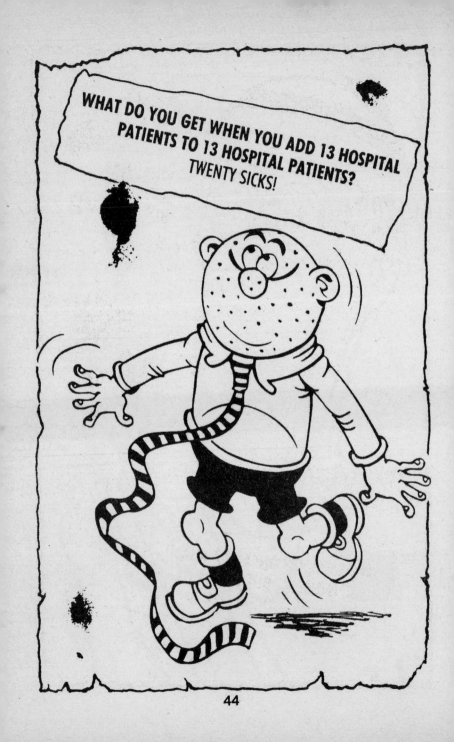

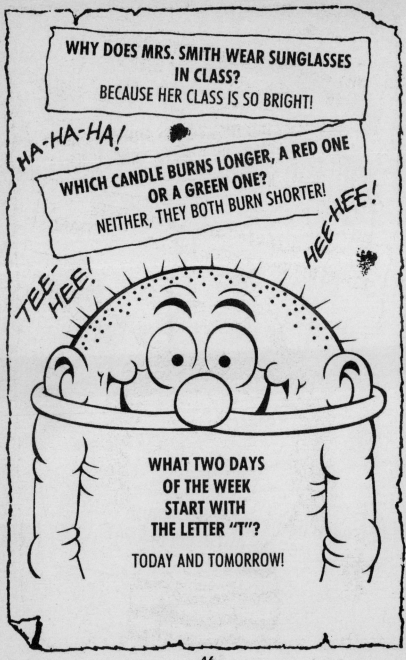

49

52

TEE-HEE!

WHAT IS BROWN, HAIRY AND
WEARS SUNGLASSES?
A COCONUT ON ITS SUMMER
HOLIDAY!

CHUCKLE CHUCKLE!

WHY CAN'T THE MAGICIAN TELL
HIS MAGIC SECRETS IN THE
GARDEN?
THE CORN HAS EARS AND THE
POTATOES HAVE EYES!

SNIGGER – SNIGGER!

WHAT DID THE MACARONI SAY TO THE TOMATO?
DON'T GET SAUCY WITH ME!

TEE-HEE!

SNIGGER-SNIGGER!

HOW DO YOU REPAIR A BROKEN TOMATO?
TOMATO PASTE!

CHORTLE! CHORTLE!

WHY DID THE BABY BISCUIT CRY?
BECAUSE HIS MUM WAS A WAFER SO LONG!

WHY DID THE BOY CLOSE THE REFRIGERATOR DOOR?
HE DIDN'T WANT TO SEE THE SALAD DRESSING!

CHUCKLE CHUCKLE!

WHAT DO YOU CALL TWO BANANA PEELS?
A PAIR OF SLIPPERS!

WHY DID THE TOMATO TURN RED?
BECAUSE HE SAW THE SALAD DRESSING!

WHAT KIND OF CAKE DO YOU GET
AT A CAFETERIA?
A STOMACH-CAKE!

WHAT TYPE OF FRUIT STEALS
HONEY?
YOGI PEAR!

WHAT IS YELLOW AND GOES
CLICK-CLICK?
A BALLPOINT BANANA!

WHERE WAS THE FIRST DOUGHNUT MADE?
IN GREASE!

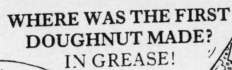

WHAT KIND OF BEAN DOESN'T GROW IN A GARDEN?
A HUMAN BEAN!

WHAT IS RED AND GOES UP AND DOWN?
A TOMATO IN A LIFT!

CHUCKLE!

HOW DO YOU TURN SOUP INTO GOLD?
PUT 14 CARROTS IN IT!

TEE-HEE!

TEE-HEE!

HOW DO YOU TEASE FRUIT?
BANANANANANANANANA!

CHORTLE!

WHAT HAPPENS WHEN YOU SIT ON A GRAPE?
IT GIVES A LITTLE WHINE!

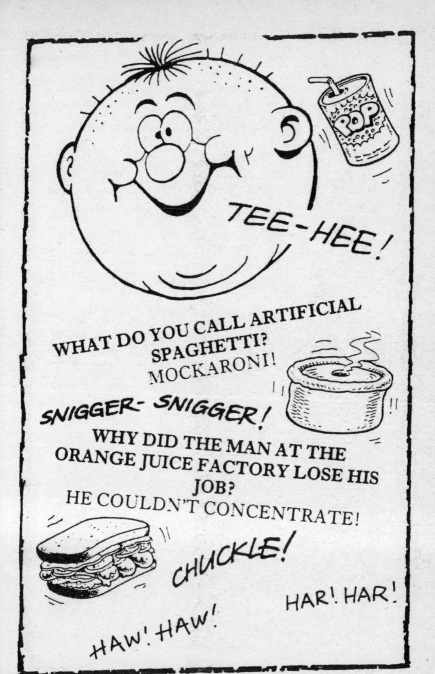

TEE-HEE!

WHAT DO YOU CALL ARTIFICIAL SPAGHETTI?
MOCKARONI!

SNIGGER- SNIGGER!

WHY DID THE MAN AT THE ORANGE JUICE FACTORY LOSE HIS JOB?
HE COULDN'T CONCENTRATE!

CHUCKLE!

HAR! HAR!

HAW! HAW!

MONSTER JOKES

WHAT DID THE BABY MONSTER
SAY TO HIS BABYSITTER?

I WANT MY MUMMY!

WHY DID THE SEA MONSTER
EAT 5 SHIPS THAT WERE
CARRYING POTATOES?

**NOBODY CAN EAT JUST ONE
POTATO SHIP!**

WHERE DOES A GHOST GO ON SATURDAY NIGHTS?
SOMEWHERE HE CAN BOOGIE!

WHAT IS A SPOOK'S FAVOURITE RIDE?
A ROLLER-GHOSTER!

70

HOW DO YOU KNOW
WHEN A GHOST
IS SAD?

HE SAYS BOOOOOOOOO
HOOOOOOOOO!

WHAT IS A MUMMY'S FAVOURITE
KIND OF MUSIC?

(W)RAP!

WHAT DOES A GHOST DO WHEN HE GETS IN A CAR?
PUTS HIS SHEET BELT ON!

WHAT DO SEA MONSTERS EAT FOR LUNCH?
POTATO SHIPS!

WHAT DID ONE GHOST SAY TO THE OTHER?
DON'T SPOOK UNTIL YOU'RE SPOOKEN TO!

WHO DID THE MONSTER TAKE TO THE HALLOWEEN DANCE?
HIS GHOUL FRIEND!

WHAT DO YOU CALL A 10 FOOT TALL MONSTER?
SHORTY!

WHAT IS THE BEST WAY TO CALL
FRANKENSTEIN'S MONSTER?
LONG DISTANCE!

WHAT IS DRACULA'S
FAVOURITE FRUIT?
NECKTARINES!

WHY DIDN'T DRACULA HAVE
MANY FRIENDS?
HE WAS A PAIN IN THE NECK!

WHAT DID THE VAMPIRE SAY
WHEN HE WAS DONE
BITING SOMEONE?
ITS BEEN NICE GNAWING YOU!

WHAT IS A VAMPIRE'S
FAVOURITE TYPE OF BOAT?
BLOOD VESSELS!

WHAT IS DRACULA'S FAVOURITE
PLACE IN NEW YORK?
THE VAMPIRE STATE BUILDING!

SPORTS JOKES

WHY IS CINDERELLA A POOR
BASKETBALL PLAYER?
BECAUSE SHE HAD A PUMPKIN
FOR A COACH!

WHY ARE FOOTBALL PLAYERS
SUCH MESSY EATERS?
BECAUSE THEY DRIBBLE!

WHY WERE THE BASKETBALL PLAYERS SO HOT AND SWEATY? BECAUSE THEIR FANS WENT AWAY!

WHY DIDN'T THE NOSE MAKE THE VOLLEYBALL TEAM?
HE DIDN'T GET PICKED!

WHY DID THE WRESTLERS PLAY IN THE DARK?
BECAUSE THEIR MATCH WOULDN'T LIGHT!

WHY DID THE CAMPERS BRING A BASEBALL PLAYER WITH THEM?
TO PITCH THE TENT!

ELEPHANT JOKES

HA-HA-HA!

WHY IS AN ELEPHANT SO WRINKLED?
BECAUSE IT'S TOO BIG TO FIT ON AN IRONING BOARD!

HA-HA-HA!

WHY DID THE ELEPHANT PAINT HIS TOENAILS RED?
SO HE COULD HIDE IN THE CHERRY TREE!

HOW DO YOU GET DOWN FROM AN ELEPHANT?
YOU DON'T, YOU GET DOWN FROM A DUCK!

WHAT HAPPENED TO RAY WHEN HE WAS STEPPED ON BY AN ELEPHANT?
HE BECAME AN X-RAY!

WHY DID THE ELEPHANT HAVE A ROTTEN HOLIDAY? THE AIRLINE LOST HIS TRUNK!

HOW DO YOU FIT AN ELEPHANT INTO A MATCHBOX? TAKE OUT THE MATCHES!

WHY CAN'T AN ELEPHANT
RIDE A TRICYCLE?
BECAUSE THEY DON'T HAVE
THUMBS TO RING THE BELL!

WHY DON'T ELEPHANTS LIKE
PLAYING CARDS IN THE JUNGLE?
BECAUSE OF ALL THE CHEETAHS!

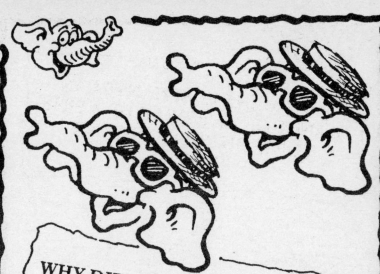

WHY DID THE TWIN ELEPHANTS GET KICKED OFF THE BEACH? BECAUSE THEY ONLY HAD ONE PAIR OF "TRUNKS"!

WHAT DO A GRAPE AND AN ELEPHANT HAVE IN COMMON? THEY'RE BOTH PURPLE, EXCEPT FOR THE ELEPHANT!

WHAT DO YOU GET WHEN YOU CROSS A SPIDER AND AN ELEPHANT?
I DON'T KNOW, BUT IF IT CRAWLS ON THE CEILING YOUR ROOF WILL COLLAPSE!

WHAT IS GREY AND HAS A TRUNK?
AN ELEPHANT ON HOLIDAY!

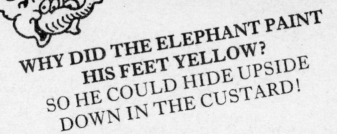

WHY DID THE ELEPHANT PAINT
HIS FEET YELLOW?
SO HE COULD HIDE UPSIDE
DOWN IN THE CUSTARD!

**WHAT DO YOU DO WHEN AN
ELEPHANT STUBS HIS TOE?**
CALL A TOE TRUCK!

**WHAT TIME IS IT WHEN AN
ELEPHANT SITS ON YOUR FENCE?**
TIME TO FIX THE FENCE!

WHY IS A SNAIL STRONGER THAN AN ELEPHANT?
A SNAIL CARRIES ITS HOUSE, AND AN ELEPHANT ONLY CARRIES HIS TRUNK!

WHY IS AN ELEPHANT LARGE, GREY AND WRINKLED?
BECAUSE IF IT WAS SMALL, WHITE AND SMOOTH IT WOULD BE AN ASPIRIN!

WHAT IS GREY WITH 16 WHEELS?
AN ELEPHANT ON ROLLER
SKATES!

WHAT DO YOU GET IF YOU CROSS
A JAGUAR AND AN ELEPHANT?
A CAR WITH A BIG TRUNK!

DID YOU KNOW THAT ELEPHANTS
NEVER FORGET?
WHAT DO THEY HAVE TO
REMEMBER?

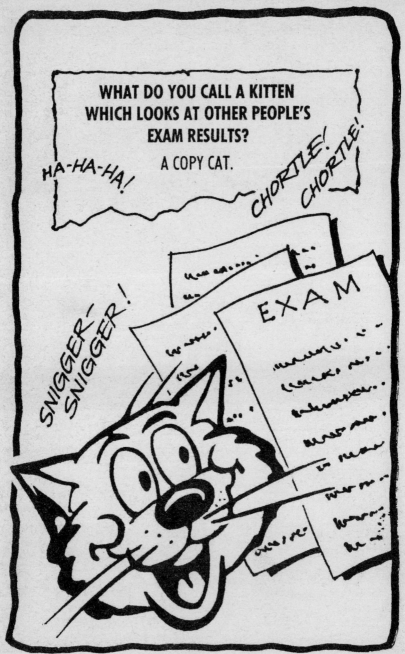